21ST-CENTURY ECONOMICS

UNDERSTANDING
TAXATION

CHET'LA SEBREE

Cavendish
Square

New York

Published in 2020 by Cavendish Square Publishing, LLC
243 5th Avenue, Suite 136, New York, NY 10016

Copyright © 2020 by Cavendish Square Publishing, LLC

First Edition

Website: cavendishsq.com

This publication represents the opinions and views of the author based on
his or her personal experience, knowledge, and research. The information
in this book serves as a general guide only. The author and publisher
have used their best efforts in preparing this book and disclaim liability
rising directly or indirectly from the use and application of this book.

All websites were available and accurate when this book was sent to press.

Library of Congress Cataloging-in-Publication Data

Names: Sebree, Chet'la, author.
Title: Understanding taxation / Chet'la Sebree.
Description: First edition. | New York : Cavendish Square, 2020. |
Series: 21st-century economics | Includes bibliographical references and index.
Identifiers: LCCN 2019005135 (print) | LCCN 2019007371 (ebook) |
ISBN 9781502646163 (ebook) | ISBN 9781502646156 (library bound) |
ISBN 9781502646149 (pbk.)
Subjects: LCSH: Taxation--United States--Juvenile literature.
Classification: LCC HJ2381 (ebook) | LCC HJ2381 .S425 2020 (print) |
DDC 336.200973--dc23
LC record available at https://lccn.loc.gov/2019005135

Editorial Director: David McNamara
Copy Editor: Nathan Heidelberger
Associate Art Director: Alan Sliwinski
Designer: Joe Parenteau
Production Coordinator: Karol Szymczuk
Photo Research: J8 Media

Portions of this book originally appeared in *How Taxation Works* by Laura La Bella.

Printed in the United States of America

CONTENTS

UNDERSTANDING TAXES

Perhaps you'll start your first job this summer. Before your first paycheck as a lifeguard, waitress, or employee in a store or amusement park, you might try to calculate how much you'll be making by multiplying your hourly rate by the number of hours you work. But when you look at your pay stub, you'll soon learn that you won't bring home every dollar you so carefully calculated. Don't worry. Your employer probably didn't forget to pay you. Instead, you are learning about an important responsibility that comes with having a job: paying taxes.

Opposite: Each paycheck you receive, whether it's for washing dishes or working as a camp counselor, will be taxed.

ings Infor...

mal Gross
uctions
itions
rtime

EARNINGS TOTAL

-Taxable Gross
able Gross

atutory & Other Deduc

eral Withholding
litional Federal Withholdi
te Withholding
litional State Withholding
;DI

Your paystub will tell you how much money
you've made so far during the year. It also
shows how much money you've paid in
different types of taxes, like income tax.

urance

rnate Retirement

Paying Taxes

You probably knew that when people worked, they had
to pay taxes. There's no doubt you've heard your parents
or grandparents complain about them. Your paycheck
will show you that if there's one thing you can't escape,

	Year to Date
.30	
0.00	
0.00	
0.00	
9.30	5,277.30
1.14	418.18
1.12	4,859.12

Current	Year to Date
311.17	311.17
0.00	*****
135.96	135.96
0.00	*****
0.00	55.06
62.67	75.55
0.00	0.00
0.00	0.00
351.14	351.14
0.00	0.00
0.00	
67.04	0.00

it's taxes. Everyone pays them. No matter how old you are, what you do for a living, or where you live, you will pay taxes in the United States. Income tax is probably the easiest to understand. When you have a job and you are making money, a portion of your income is likely withheld to pay taxes.

While even in Monopoly you pay an income tax, not all states actually have this type of tax at the state level.

But there are many different types of taxes in the United States. You will pay separate taxes to the federal government and to the state government in which you live. Plus, you may pay taxes to your local government (the town, city, or county you live in). You'll also pay for services you might not even understand yet, like Social Security and Medicare/Medicaid.

Where Does the Money Go?

While it can be frustrating to see your hard-earned money go somewhere other than in your pocket, taxation is an important part of government. For instance, the US government acts as a very large business with a lot of debt and expenses. Many of those expenses are services citizens of the United States get to use, such as public assistance like food stamps and education. Other services, like the military, keep the country safe during times of war and peace. To handle these costs, the government needed to create revenue, or income.

Citizens in most countries pay taxes their entire lives. For that reason, it's important to understand how taxes work, what kinds of taxes we pay, why we pay them, where the money goes, and who spends our tax dollars. It can help you to better prepare for your future if you have a fuller understanding of taxes.

CHAPTER 1

DIFFERENT TYPES OF TAXES

Although you may not understand them, you've probably heard people talk about taxes quite a bit. You've probably heard your parents at dinner or politicians on television talking about high or low taxes. You're also affected by them when you make purchases. For instance, depending on which state you live in, video games, books, groceries, and clothes are taxed. You might be asking yourself why we pay taxes. How can a few cents added to the purchase of *Harry Potter* be that important? Learning about taxes and why we pay them is important to understanding how our government works.

Opposite: In some states, there is a type of tax called sales tax. This means that buyers pay a certain percentage in taxes for items they purchase, like books or video games.

The Basics

In its simplest form, a government determines the way in which a country, state, county, town, city, or village is run. At every level of government, laws are created that citizens must obey. Policies are put in place for just about everything connected with our daily lives. A community

American colonists were frustrated by the taxation imposed on them by the British, especially since there wasn't anyone representing the colonists' interests in the British government.

needs an organized way to function, and a government provides that framework.

The US government provides public goods and services for the citizens of the country as a whole. But since the government doesn't generate any income of its own, it needs a way to pay its bills. The money that the US government uses to pay these bills comes mostly from taxes.

Taxes have been a part of US history since its earliest days. In fact, taxation forced on the colonists by the British government was one of the reasons the colonists fought for independence in the first place. However, when writing the Constitution, the Founding Fathers knew that the young country would need the money generated from taxes to help build the country's infrastructure, or the fundamental systems that manage the country. The government generated this money by taxing imports and certain purchases like alcohol.

OK, but What Are Taxes?

Simply put, the government charges its citizens taxes, which pay for services such as the US Postal Service or the public education system. They also go toward paying the salaries and benefits of the armed forces.

There are two main groups that collect taxes: the federal government and state governments. The federal government taxes people by using a universal chart based

WHO MANAGES THE MONEY?

When you pay taxes, the money goes to two places. The federal government and your state government both collect the taxes they charge on your income or on purchases you make at stores. The Internal Revenue Service (IRS) is a federal government agency that is responsible for collecting taxes. These taxes fund federal services such as the military and homeland security. Taxes also support offices that have certain responsibilities, like the Department of Education, which supports student achievement and educational excellence, and the National Aeronautics and Space Administration (NASA). Running the federal government itself costs money, too. Everyone from the president of the United States to the staffers that work in government agencies are employed by the US government. Their salaries and the costs of running each of these offices are also paid with the taxes collected from citizens.

Most state governments that collect taxes send the money to a taxation department. This office is responsible

The money collected by the IRS goes to the US Department of the Treasury, which is responsible for managing the country's revenue.

for collecting taxes and distributing the money to state agencies to be spent on services for the public. State taxes help pay for public schools, police, state-run colleges and universities, statewide roads and highway systems, and health and public services.

on a person's income. The chart is the same no matter which state you live in.

State taxes work a little bit differently. Each state government can set its own tax rate, or the amount of taxes people pay. These rates can differ widely from state to state. Citizens pay state taxes in addition to the taxes they pay to the federal government. The reason for this is that each state offers services that are different from the services offered by the federal government. For example, federal taxes pay for the military when the United States goes to war. However, state taxes pay for services available in your state. For instance, state taxes help to cover expenses related to public transportation and state prisons. The availability of these types of services is dependent on state taxes.

Tax Collection

There are a number of ways the government collects taxes. We pay different types of taxes depending on our income, the kinds of purchases we make, and whether we own property or a home. The amount we pay in taxes varies as well. We may pay a higher tax on our income than we do for a clothing purchase at the mall. Among the most common types of taxes Americans pay are income taxes, Social Security taxes, sales taxes, property taxes, and excise taxes.

Income Taxes

As its name suggests, income tax is tax that you pay on the money you earn from your job or investments, known as your income. Businesses also pay taxes on the money they make from selling goods and services. This type of income tax is called a corporate tax. A good percentage of Americans pay federal income tax, and forty-three of fifty states charge their residents a state income tax.

The United States has what is called a progressive tax system. This means that the more money a person makes, the higher his or her tax rate is. Someone who makes very little money pays a lower tax rate than someone who earns a very high income. Federal tax rates appear in a chart that assigns a tax rate to your income bracket. An income tax bracket is a category based on how much money you make.

In 2019, there were seven different tax brackets with the following tax rates: 10, 12, 22, 24, 32, 35, and 37 percent. These brackets are affected by whether you are single, married filing jointly (filing taxes together on one tax form), or married filing separately. For example, in 2019 if you were a single person earning less than $9,700 each year, you would have fallen in the 10 percent tax bracket. This means that you would have paid 10 percent of your income in taxes. However, if you were married, you would fall in the 10 percent tax

Table 1. Tax Brackets and Rates, 2019

Rate	For Unmarried Individuals, Taxable Income Over	For Married Individuals Filing Joint Returns, Taxable Income Over	For Heads of Households, Taxable Income Over
10%	$0	$0	$0
12%	$9,700	$19,400	$13,850
22%	$39,475	$78,950	$52,850
24%	$84,200	$168,400	$84,200
32%	$160,725	$321,450	$160,700
35%	$204,100	$408,200	$204,100
37%	$510,300	$612,350	$510,300

The federal government adjusts the tax brackets each year in response to the cost of living.

bracket if you and your partner filed together and made less than $19,400.

It can be hard to understand how your total taxes are calculated because you actually pay taxes at a given rate only for each dollar that falls within that bracket's range. For example, if you as a single person earn $10,700 in a year, the first $9,700 will be taxed at the 10 percent rate. However, the last $1,000 will be taxed at the 12 percent rate. Many states have a similar progressive income tax, while other states have a flat tax.

When you receive a paycheck, you may also pay state taxes on the money you've made. This is in addition to paying the federal income tax. There are only seven states that do not have a state income tax. They are: Alaska,

Florida, Nevada, South Dakota, Texas, Washington, and Wyoming. Residents of New Hampshire and Tennessee also don't have to pay income taxes on their paychecks. They do, however, pay taxes on income from investments. In general, states with income taxes tax their residents at a much lower rate than the federal government does.

Some towns and cities also impose local income taxes on their citizens. Again, this tax would be in addition to the federal and state income taxes you might pay. For example, in 2018, New York State's income tax ranged between 4 and 8.82 percent, depending on residents' tax brackets. New York City, however, had an additional local income tax of between 2.907 and 3.876 percent. These local income taxes help pay for local services, such as snow removal in the winter, public schools, and police and fire departments.

Social Security Taxes

When you review your paycheck, you will see the amount of money you pay toward federal and state taxes listed on the pay stub. You might also see the word "FICA" next to a small amount of money that has also been withheld from your pay. This is the amount of money you pay in Social Security taxes. Also known as the Federal Insurance Contributions Act (FICA) tax, this tax helps fund Social Security and Medicare.

Social Security refers to a social insurance program that was created by the US government to protect its citizens against the effects of poverty, old age, disability, and unemployment. For instance, once you are sixty-two or older you can apply for Social Security benefits. Based on your age, the years you worked, and your salary when you were working, you will receive a monthly check from the government. The government distributes this money from the pot it has collected from people paying their Social Security taxes. Medicare, a health insurance program for people over the age of sixty-five, works in a similar capacity. It is partially funded through payroll taxes.

Sales Tax

State and local governments impose a sales tax to raise money for local projects like building libraries and funding prisons. The rate varies from state to state, county to county, and city to city. Sales tax is imposed on items you buy from stores, such as clothing, shoes, furniture, and electronics. Food purchases at restaurants are often taxable, but food purchased at a grocery store may be exempt, meaning it isn't taxed.

Sales tax is called a flat tax, meaning that everyone pays the same amount of tax on an item. This tax is not based on your income. Even if you make more money,

SHOPPING STORE

03:22 PM
618

REG 12-21
CLERK 2

1 MISC. $0.49
1 STUFF $7.99
  SUBTOTAL $8.48
  TAX $0.22
  TOTAL $9. $10.00
  CASH $0.78
  CHANGE

NO REFUNDS
NO EXCHANGES
NO RETURNS

When you see "tax" listed on a receipt for an item you've purchased at the store, this reflects the state's sales tax.

you will pay the same amount of tax on a sweater as someone who makes much less money than you do.

Property Taxes

Property taxes are taxes that you pay on real estate. Taxes on land, and the buildings on it, are the biggest source of revenue for local governments. The village, town, city, or county where your property is located is in charge of collecting these taxes. Your local government decides the value of your real estate, such as your home, your business, or any other property you might own. Then, it determines how much money you should pay in property taxes. The money the local government raises is usually used for building and supporting local infrastructure. Property owners pay property taxes annually.

Excise Taxes

Excise taxes are additional taxes people pay for items such as alcohol, tobacco, and gambling. Excise taxes can affect the economy and influence consumer behavior. An excise tax is used to discourage the use of products and services that could pose a risk to someone's health, such as alcohol or tobacco. In the case of cigarettes, in 2018 the federal excise tax was $1.0066 for each pack of cigarettes. People also pay a state tax, which varies depending on where you live.

In addition to a federal excise tax on cigarettes, there are other excise taxes that vary from state to state and from city to city. People in New York City, for instance, pay a federal, state, and local tax on cigarettes.

On average, the excise tax for cigarettes is $1.70. However, some states have much higher or much lower tax rates. For instance, as of 2018, Connecticut and New York both charged $4.35 per pack in state taxes. These two states had the highest tax rates, followed closely by Rhode Island, with a $4.25 tax rate. Other states, however, like Georgia, Virginia, and Missouri, had much lower rates: $0.37, $0.30, and $0.17, respectively, in 2018. Some places, like New York City, also charge an additional local tax on them.

Direct Versus Indirect Taxes

With all of these different types of taxes, it might be hard to understand when and how to pay them. A direct tax is one that the taxpayer pays directly to the government. These taxes include income tax, Social Security tax, sales tax, property tax, and excise tax. These taxes cannot be shifted to others. An indirect tax is one that is passed on to another person or group. Fuel for our cars is an example of a tax passed on to consumers. The cost of fuel includes a tax that consumers pay, which raises the price of gasoline. Instead of oil companies paying that tax, they pass it on to consumers.

Knowledge about the different types of taxes and how to pay them helps with understanding taxes. Learning a little about the history of taxation can help as well.

CHAPTER 2

THE HISTORY OF US TAXES

Taxation in the United States dates back to colonial times and the earliest days of the country's history. In fact, taxes were one of the main reasons the American colonists fought for independence from England. The US tax system, which includes federal, state, and local taxes, has changed many times throughout the nation's history. There have been times when taxes have been raised to help pay for wars and times when taxes have been lowered to help build the economy.

Taxation and Representation

Taxes are part of the fabric of US history. The Stamp Act of 1765 was the first tax imposed directly on the

Opposite: American colonists rebelled against the taxes imposed on them by the government in Great Britain.

American colonies by Great Britain. The new tax required the colonists to pay a tax on every piece of printed paper they used. This included everything from papers that accompanied shipments of goods to legal documents, licenses, newspapers, other publications, and even playing cards. Colonists disliked this tax because it was imposed by England to raise money. Until the Stamp Act, previous taxes had only been used to regulate the

This is an anti–Stamp Act political cartoon. The Stamp Act of 1765 placed a tax on all printed paper in colonial America, from legal documents to playing cards.

economy. This tax, however, was created so that Great Britain could afford its wars against France.

Colonists were also angry about the Stamp Act because it forced them to financially support a government they had no say in running. Colonists had no elected representative in the British government. This meant that people an ocean away could make decisions that affected their daily lives. This led to the rallying cry of the American Revolution: "Taxation without representation is tyranny."

While colonists fought the American Revolution, some worked to create and develop the new country's federal government. During this process, the Founding Fathers wrote the Declaration of Independence and the Articles of Confederation, which became the country's first constitution in 1781. A constitution provides a framework for the organization of a government. With the establishment of this new nation, the citizens of the United States now had proper democratic representation. However, this new government made no money of its own and relied on donations from its states to provide it with an income.

The US Constitution replaced the Articles of Confederation in 1787. The document defined the three main branches of the government: the legislative branch, the executive branch, and the judicial branch. The legislative branch includes the House of

AS OLD AS TIME

Taxation is an ancient system that can be traced back to the days of the pharaohs in Egypt and to the Roman Empire. Both civilizations collected taxes. In ancient Egypt, the tax collection system, like the United States' system, was focused on the common good. Taxes were collected and redistributed. Taxes at the time, however, were paid in grain.

Grain was needed for multiple reasons in the ancient society. It was used for construction and offerings, kept in reserves to feed people during droughts, and used for government administration. In terms of government, grain was a top commodity, or product. Egypt used it to trade with other countries, especially for resources or goods the country lacked. When tax season came, the grain was collected and redistributed according to need.

In the top-right portion of this painting that appears in an ancient Egyptian tomb, a person who has failed to pay his taxes in grain has been captured and punished.

Representatives and the Senate, collectively known as Congress. Each state elects representatives to fill positions in the House and Senate, giving each state a voice in the federal government.

When the Founding Fathers wrote the US Constitution, they knew that the country would need to raise money to build cities and create a military for protection. They also realized that the government could not function properly if it relied entirely on its states' donations for its resources. As a result, the Constitution gave Congress the power to "lay and collect taxes, duties, imposts, and excises, to pay the debts and provide for the common defense and general welfare of the United States." In other words, the federal government was granted the authority to raise money and impose taxes on the American people.

New Eras, New Taxes

As the United States has grown and evolved since it first declared independence in 1776, so have taxes. The US government has adjusted the tax system as circumstances have created the need for more money. War and times of growth and prosperity have influenced taxation. For instance, the United States first raised money from tariffs, which were the largest source of federal revenue from the 1790s to the beginning of the Civil War. A tariff is a tax imposed on goods when they are moved from one country to another. The goods cannot continue on their way until the tax is paid.

However, when the Civil War began, the US government needed more money to pay for war expenses. As a result, Congress passed the Revenue Act of 1861, which imposed a tax on personal income. This established a new direction of the country's federal tax system, as it had initially been based on excise taxes and tariffs. When it became clear that the Civil War would not end as quickly as the government thought it would, the federal government realized it would need more money. According to the US Department of the Treasury, Congress created new excise taxes on such items as gunpowder, feathers, telegrams, iron, leather, pianos, yachts, billiard tables, drugs, patent medicines, and whiskey. Many legal documents were also taxed, and license fees were collected for many professions. In fact, the Civil War led to the founding of the Bureau of Internal Revenue, which would later become the Internal Revenue Service (IRS). The IRS is responsible for tax collection.

After the Civil War ended, the government realized it didn't need as much money, so the income tax was abolished in 1872. The Spanish-American War in 1898 created a renewed need for money, so taxes were established on items such as gum and doubled on beer and tobacco. In 1913, the Sixteenth Amendment was

The Spanish-American War (1898) ended Spain's colonial rule in the Americas. The US war effort was largely funded by taxes. For instance, the Revenue Act of 1898 established a sales tax on gum.

approved. It allowed Congress to impose an income tax without having to distribute it among the states based on the size of their populations. This population-based division had previously been required by the Constitution. It had made collecting a federal income tax virtually impossible. This is because not everyone makes the same amount of money. A state with lots of rich people would end up paying a higher share of income taxes relative to its total population than a state with lots of poor people. While people had been willing to overlook this issue during the national crisis of the Civil War, later attempts to impose a federal income tax had been stopped by the Supreme Court. All of this changed in 1913 with the passage of the Sixteenth Amendment. A small federal income tax was imposed that year.

The United States' involvement in World War I greatly increased the need for revenue. Congress responded by passing the Revenue Act of 1916. The act doubled the lowest income tax rate from 1 percent to 2 percent and increased the top tax rate to 15 percent for those people who had incomes of more than $1.5 million. However, the government slowly realized two problems. There was not an organized way to collect taxes, and not everyone paid their taxes. In 1918, only 5 percent of the population paid their income taxes, and yet it was this tax that was funding one-third of the cost of the war.

After the war came to an end, the economy boomed during the Roaring Twenties. It was a time in which the United States experienced social, artistic, and cultural growth. Increases in revenues from income taxes followed as people began to make more money. The United States saw a huge growth in industry as new technologies, especially cars and movies, grew in popularity. Taxes were cut five times to encourage the growth of the economy. But all of this came crashing down on October 29, 1929, known as Black Tuesday. This was the day the stock market collapsed, plunging the country into economic despair. The event contributed to the Great Depression, when millions of people were out of work. This economic depression lasted throughout the 1930s. As the economy shrank and people lost their jobs, there was less income to tax, and the government felt the effects. Congress increased taxes to keep money coming into the government. The downside was that those who were lucky enough to have jobs saw a greater portion of their income go to the government.

When World War II broke out, the United States needed money to fund its involvement. It was a very tense time for tax policy. Everyone from the president to congressmen agreed that taxes needed to be high to create revenue to pay for the supplies the soldiers needed. In 1940, only around 10 percent of the population paid federal income

During the Great Depression, there were periods when 25 percent of white Americans and 50 percent of African Americans were unemployed. These people were unable to pay taxes.

tax. By 1944, after the United States entered the war, nearly every employed person paid income taxes. This tax money went toward soldiers' salaries, goods needed in combat, food to feed the troops, and equipment to support military efforts.

Around this time, the IRS created a "pay-as-you-go" system of tax withholding. In this system, taxes are withheld from each person's paycheck and sent to the government instead of individuals paying taxes in one lump sum each year. While the pay-as-you-go system (which is still used today) made it easier for both the taxpayer and the tax collectors, it also reduced the taxpayer's knowledge of how much money was being collected. This made it easier for the government to raise taxes without taxpayers feeling the burden immediately.

The government continued to make changes to the tax system as the country changed. In the 1980s, President Ronald Reagan drastically reduced taxes. His Economic Recovery Tax Act of 1981 reduced the amount of federal income tax for workers. When many of the tax cuts the act created went into effect, the economy began a pattern of growth that lasted throughout much of the 1980s, though economists continue to debate how much Reagan's tax policy contributed to that growth. The 1990s and 2000s saw a number of tax acts, from the Taxpayer Relief Act of 1997, which gave families a tax credit for each child in a family, to the Economic Growth and Tax Relief and Reconciliation Act of 2001, which cut taxes slightly.

During the Great Recession, a period economic downturn between 2007 and 2009, tax policies changed again to support people struggling financially. During this time, a great number of people lost their jobs and homes as companies went out of business. The Tax

Relief, Unemployment Insurance Reauthorization, and Job Creation Act of 2010 was developed to help these individuals. It cut income taxes in addition to extending unemployment insurance benefits. These benefits provided temporary financial assistance to people who lost their jobs because companies cut workers they could not afford during the recession.

Tax Policy in Real Life

Taxes will continue to change as government leaders look for ways to maintain or increase tax revenue while balancing the impact on the workers. History has shown us that as the country enters wars and periods of economic growth or depression, and as the government needs more money to fund initiatives, taxes will continue to be raised and lowered to help support various projects. These decisions have varying effects on people's pockets.

UNITED STATES

Internal
Revenue
Service
Building

← Visitors
← ♿

CHAPTER 3

THE EFFECTS: BENEFITS AND DRAWBACKS

The US federal and state governments can change taxes as often as they want. All that's needed is for a new tax bill to be passed in Congress or a state's governing body. Sometimes the government raises taxes to help pay for war or to support a struggling economy. Other times, taxes may be lowered to help taxpayers keep more money in their pockets. Taxes often change from year to year. Tax increases and tax cuts are both very common.

Tax Increases

To understand the effect of a tax increase, we need to take a look at who bears the burden of the tax. For example, suppose the price of a T-shirt is $10. The government

Opposite: The Internal Revenue Service is not only responsible for collecting federal taxes but for enforcing the tax codes created by Congress.

imposes a 10 percent tax on T-shirt sellers for each T-shirt. A few weeks after the tax goes into effect, it causes the price of a T-shirt to increase to $11. The T-shirt sellers receive the same amount per T-shirt as they did before the tax, so the tax increase has not affected the sellers. Instead, consumers pay the entire tax in the form of higher prices. What if taxes are increased from 10 percent to 15 percent per T-shirt? That $10 T-shirt now costs $11.50. Would you buy it now that it costs more due to an increase in taxes? Perhaps. But imagine the difference in prices for much larger purchases, like cars or boats. Imagine you want to buy a new luxury car. The base cost is $40,000. With a 10 percent tax, the car costs $44,000. However, with a 15 percent tax, the car costs $46,000—a much more dramatic difference than the extra $1.50 you would pay for a T-shirt with the same tax rate.

Tax Cuts

A tax cut is a reduction in taxes. When a tax cut occurs, the government sees a decrease in the income it receives from taxes. Those who pay taxes see an increase in the amount of money they get to keep from their paycheck. Sometimes when taxpayers receive more money from a tax cut, they decide to spend it. This helps the economy grow because businesses do well when people spend money. The businesses might be inclined to hire more people, which would lead to more income tax that the government could collect. Additionally, when people purchase more products, they pay more in local and state taxes, such as sales tax. But when the economy is bad and there is a tax cut, some people tend to save any extra money they receive. While people have more money to spend, they are scared to spend it because they are unsure of what lies ahead. They think they might need that extra money in the future. This hurts the economy.

Government Spending

The federal budget of the US government is created by the president of the United States and is sent to the US Congress at the beginning of the year, in January or February. Members of the Senate and the House of Representatives make additional recommendations after they review the budget. Congress then sends the budget back to the president for approval. Once the president approves the budget, it goes into effect on October 1 each year. Certain parts of the budget are mandatory expenses, such as Social Security and Medicare. But other spending is flexible. The government must decide what to fund and what it may hold off on funding until the following year. Sometimes money is taken away from one area to support another. When the United States is at war, military spending increases. Cuts might be made to other areas to help work toward a balanced budget and control overspending. Sometimes, Congress and the president cannot agree on the budget. For instance, in December 2018, parts of the federal government shut down, or stopped operating at their full capacity, because Congress and President Donald Trump disagreed over the budget. President Trump wanted $5.7 billion to build a wall on the United States' southern border with Mexico—money that would come out of taxpayers' pockets. Congress refused to support his desire for a wall, proposing different types of border security.

These are the types of projects, however, that taxpayers' dollars can go toward. When the federal government collects taxes, it uses them to pay for expenses that keep the government running and for projects it deems essential to national security. Each year, the federal government creates a budget and makes it available for citizens to see. You might be wondering what the US government spends tax dollars on. The following are just a few examples of the types of programs the taxes the government collects support.

Federal Debt

The federal government has debt, and a lot of it. The government takes on debt when it spends more than it receives in taxes. At the end of 2017, the United States was $20.4 trillion in debt. Taxes help pay off the debt the government owes to investors and foreign governments.

Social Security and Medicare

Retired people are eligible to collect Social Security once they reach a certain age. We each pay Social Security taxes in the hopes that one day we will receive this money back to help support us as we age.

Additionally, taxpayer dollars support Medicare, which is a health insurance program. Medicare specifically supports people over the age of sixty-five and some people who are younger who have disabilities or who are in kidney failure.

Health Research

Keeping our nation healthy is important. Our taxes fund the Food and Drug Administration (FDA) and dozens of programs that keep our citizens healthy like the Centers for Disease Control and Prevention (CDC). The FDA regulates the safety and efficacy of new drugs. The federal agency also makes sure food is up to safety standards, which helps prevent food-borne illnesses. Similarly, the CDC, as its name suggests, tries to protect people against the spread of diseases. Less obviously, it also strives to ensure workplace safety.

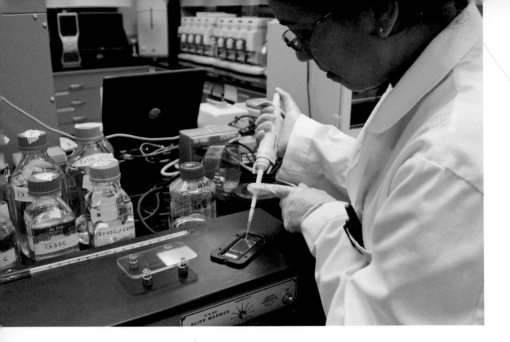

The research conducted by the Food and Drug Administration (FDA) is funded through tax dollars.

Defense

Taxpayer dollars cover everything from military salaries to wars in foreign countries to the research, development, and purchase of new military technologies. Additionally, the federal government provides income and health benefits to veterans, people who previously fought in wars or worked for our military.

Low-Income Programs

Some tax dollars go toward programs for those who need financial help to support themselves and their families. These programs include food stamps, housing support, and childcare assistance.

Education

Primarily, states cover the majority of education costs for local schools. The US government, however, contributes to programs for low-income school districts, special education, and financial aid programs for college students.

Community Development

In the event of a major natural disaster, the Federal Emergency Management Agency (FEMA) assists people in rebuilding their lives and communities. For instance, FEMA stepped in after Hurricane Katrina destroyed much of New Orleans, Louisiana.

The Federal Emergency Management Agency (FEMA) supports citizens affected by disasters on US soil.

Highways and Public Transit

Most highway and mass-transit spending is supported by the taxes we pay. This includes roads, bridges, and bus and subway systems.

Prisons

Taxes also support prisons and law enforcement programs.

International Affairs

The funding for international affairs includes the operation of US embassies and consulates abroad and contributions to organizations such as the United Nations. US embassies and consulates support Americans traveling and living abroad. For instance, if you misplaced your passport while in another country, you would go to one of these offices for support.

Agriculture

Farms may receive assistance from the government to be successful or to stay in operation. This is important because people rely on the farm industry for food like meat and produce. The government works to make sure that farmers can continue to make enough of a profit to keep farming.

Can We Eliminate Taxes?

Getting rid of taxes altogether has been a proposed idea for some time. While people would earn more money and their purchasing ability would increase, federal and state governments wouldn't earn any income from taxation and couldn't pay for services that are shared by everyone.

Without taxes, a country might not have the money to defend itself against war or provide even the most basic of services. The government would not be able to function if we did not support the people who run it. Local services used by those in need (e.g., public assistance, police, and firefighters) would need to be paid for by individuals, who likely could not afford them. Many services would simply disappear. There would be no maintenance on roads or bridges, and snow would not be removed in the winter months. If part of our country was struck by a natural disaster, no aid would be available to help the people in those communities rebuild.

Tax Resistance and Evasion

Despite the wide acceptance of the need for taxation, some people still actively disagree. Some people even refuse to pay their taxes. Tax resisters decide they no longer want to pay taxes because they disagree with how

Al Capone was a notorious gangster. Although he was guilty of many crimes, such as murder, he was only ever convicted for tax evasion.

tax revenues are being spent or feel tax rates are unfair. Some protest the idea of taxes, and others even refuse to pay in an attempt to damage or overthrow a government. Refusing to pay your taxes is a risky thing to do and can result in penalties that include high fines and possibly time in prison.

Tax evasion is when people use illegal means to avoid paying taxes they owe. Failing to file a tax return, failing to report all of one's income, or concealing income earned illegally (through gambling, theft, etc.) are all forms of tax evasion. Tax evasion is a serious crime and brings with it serious penalties. The IRS can fine a person for evading taxes. The fine includes the amount the person owes the government, plus a penalty amount that can total thousands of dollars. The IRS can also send you to prison for up to five years for avoiding filing your tax return. A tax return is a document that shows the federal and state governments what you are declaring as taxable. For example, taxable items on your income tax return include your salary, tips, and any income from a house or any property you own, such as rent paid to you.

QUICK Q&A

Do I have to file taxes if I'm a student?

Yes! Many people believe that students don't have to file a tax return or pay their taxes. But that's untrue. Students must pay taxes on their income and file a tax return. Students do get special tax credits and can deduct some of their educational expenses, which may lower their tax bill.

How do I determine much money comes out of my paychecks for income tax?

When you start a new job, your employer will ask you to provide information on a form called a W-4. This form helps your employer determine how much money to withhold from your wages and how much to pay to the government on your behalf. It is important to fill out your form accurately and completely.

What happens after I file my tax return?

When you file your taxes, you should keep your records in a safe location for at least seven years. It's possible that you could be audited. This means that the IRS will review your taxes and records for up to three years after you file your tax return. Should you ever be audited, having your past financial records and a copy of your tax forms is crucial.

Form **1040**

Department of the Treasury—Internal Revenue Service (99)

U.S. Individual Income Tax Return 2015 OMB No. 1545-0074 | IRS Use Only—Do not write or staple in this space.

For the year Jan. 1–Dec. 31, 2015, or other tax year beginning _____ , 2015, ending _____ , 20 ___ | See separate instructions.

Your first name and initial	Last name		Your social security number
If a joint return, spouse's first name and initial	Last name		Spouse's social security number

Home address (number and street). If you have a P.O. box, see instructions. | Apt. no.

▲ Make sure the SSN(s) above and on line 6c are correct.

City, town or post office, state, and ZIP code. If you have a foreign address, also complete spaces below (see instructions).

Presidential Election Campaign
Check here if you, or your spouse if filing jointly, want $3 to go to this fund. Checking a box below will not change your tax or refund. ☐ You ☐ Spouse

Foreign country name | Foreign province/state/county | Foreign postal code

Filing Status

Check only one box.

1 ☐ Single
2 ☐ Married filing jointly (even if only one had income)
3 ☐ Married filing separately. Enter spouse's SSN above and full name here. ▶
4 ☐ Head of household (with qualifying person). (See instructions.) If the qualifying person is a child but not your dependent, enter this child's name here. ▶
5 ☐ Qualifying widow(er) with dependent child

Exemptions

6a ☐ Yourself. If someone can claim you as a dependent, **do not check box 6a.**
b ☐ Spouse
c Dependents:

(1) First name Last name	(2) Dependent's social security number	(3) Dependent's relationship to you	(4) ✓ if child under age 17 qualifying for child tax credit (see instructions)
			☐
			☐
			☐
			☐

If more than four dependents, see instructions and check here ▶ ☐

d Total number of exemptions claimed

Boxes checked on 6a and 6b _____
No. of children on 6c who:
• lived with you _____
• did not live with you due to divorce or separation (see instructions) _____
Dependents on 6c not entered above _____
Add numbers on lines above ▶ _____

Income

Attach Form(s) W-2 here. Also attach Forms W-2G and 1099-R if tax was withheld.

If you did not get a W-2, see instructions.

7	Wages, salaries, tips, etc. Attach Form(s) W-2		7
8a	Taxable interest. Attach Schedule B if required		8a
b	Tax-exempt interest. **Do not include on line 8a**	8b	
9a	Ordinary dividends. Attach Schedule B if required		9a
b	Qualified dividends	9b	
10	Taxable refunds, credits, or offsets of state and local income taxes		10
11	Alimony received		11
12	Business income or (loss). Attach Schedule C or C-EZ		12
13	Capital gain or (loss). Attach Schedule D if required. If not required, check here ▶ ☐		13
14	Other gains or (losses). Attach Form 4797		14
15a	IRA distributions 15a	b Taxable amount	15b
16a	Pensions and annuities 16a	b Taxable amount	16b
17	Rental real estate, royalties, partnerships, S corporations, trusts, etc. Attach Schedule E		17
18	Farm income or (loss). Attach Schedule F		18
19	Unemployment compensation		19
20a	Social security benefits 20a	b Taxable amount	20b
21	Other income. List type and amount		21
22	Combine the amounts in the far right column for lines 7 through 21. This is your **total income** ▶		22

Adjusted Gross Income

23	Educator expenses	23	
24	Certain business expenses of reservists, performing artists, and fee-basis government officials. Attach Form 2106 or 2106-EZ	24	
25	Health savings account deduction. Attach Form 8889	25	
26	Moving expenses. Attach Form 3903	26	
27	Deductible part of self-employment tax. Attach Schedule SE	27	
28	Self-employed SEP, SIMPLE, and qualified plans	28	
29	Self-employed health insurance deduction	29	
30	Penalty on early withdrawal of savings	30	
31a	Alimony paid b Recipient's SSN ▶	31a	
32	IRA deduction	32	
33	Student loan interest deduction	33	
34	Tuition and fees. Attach Form 8917	34	
35	Domestic production activities deduction. Attach Form 8903	35	
36	Add lines 23 through 35		36
37	Subtract line 36 from line 22. This is your adjusted gross income ▶		37

For Disclosure, Privacy Act, and Paperwork Reduction Act Notice, see separate instructions. | Cat. No. 11320B | Form **1040** (2015)

CHAPTER 4

TAX RETURNS

As a taxpayer, you are responsible for paying your taxes and filing a tax return. Everyone who earns a certain amount of income must file a federal tax return, which shows the federal government both how much money you earned and how much you have paid in taxes. The federal government then reviews these forms and notifies you if you have paid too much in taxes or not enough. If you paid too much in taxes, you will get money returned to you. This is called a refund. If you have not paid enough, you will be told how much more you need to pay. Filing with states that impose an income tax works in a similar way.

Opposite: Most taxpayers will fill out Form 1040 for their federal income tax return.

Filing Tax Returns

In the United States, all tax forms are due to the federal and state governments by April 15 of each year, unless this date falls on a weekend. Since computers are now used to help calculate tax forms, you can file your forms electronically, which saves time, paper, and money.

The United States' tax system is a voluntary system. This means it is each taxpayer's responsibility to volunteer, or report, information about all of his or her income. As a taxpayer, you have responsibilities, which include knowing when and where to file your tax returns, keeping accurate and complete records of your income, and giving the government (federal and state) accurate information on your tax returns. It is against the law to fail to report your income. It is called tax evasion. Tax evasion is a serious crime. When people do not pay their taxes, the government loses money.

While taxpayers have a responsibility to file an accurate and timely tax return, they also have certain rights that protect them and the personal information they share with the federal and state governments. All taxpayers have the right to privacy of their tax information. Only authorized tax personnel can examine, or audit, a tax return. Even law enforcement agencies have no right to examine a person's tax returns. In addition, taxpayers have the right to appeal any IRS-proposed adjustments to a tax return or contest the results of an audit.

Audits

Annually, the IRS conducts audits. A tax audit is an investigation into the tax documents filed by a person or corporation. Audits are used to ensure that tax documents are completed correctly and that all taxes that a person or corporation should be paying are actually submitted. Generally, a computer selects tax returns at random for auditing. However, the IRS also conducts audits if it detects unusual activity.

The IRS only audited 0.5 percent of tax returns filed for the year 2016. This means that out of about 196 million tax returns filed, only about 1.1 million were audited. In perhaps more digestible terms, this means that if you had about two hundred friends, only one of you would be audited. That's a fairly small number.

The Logistics

You can file your tax return a couple of ways. You can file electronically using a computer, or you can fill out the forms by hand and mail them into the IRS and your state's revenue department using the US Postal Service. There are key benefits to electronically preparing and filing your tax returns. These include increased accuracy, faster refunds, and the ability to file your federal and state returns simultaneously. People filing taxes can either fill out the forms (electronically or on paper) themselves or hire a professional.

Completing the forms yourself often requires the use of tax preparation software and a personal computer. The software gives taxpayers access to the latest rules and regulations. Also, using a computer enables taxpayers to transmit their returns from home, their workplace, or a library.

Many people leave the task of completing tax forms to professional tax advisers or accountants when it is time to file their annual tax returns. Hiring someone means giving a tax professional your information. The tax expert then calculates your taxes on your behalf. Tax professionals can include certified public accountants (CPAs), tax attorneys, IRS-enrolled agents, or tax preparation businesses. Tax professionals charge a fee for preparing your taxes. Choosing the right person for the job is important. You should look for someone who is knowledgeable about your state's tax policies and who will support you if the IRS decides to select your tax documents for audit.

Calculating Tax Liability

Federal income tax is based on a percentage of your personal income. The federal government uses a chart

Hiring a tax professional can have many benefits. For instance, many tax professionals promise that they'll help you if you are audited by the IRS.

that everyone follows. The chart shows the percentage of a person's income that he or she would pay based on how much he or she makes. The more money someone makes, the higher the tax he or she pays. For those states that have an income tax, the tax is based on a percentage of your income as well.

The amount of your income that is taxed, however, is dependent on your tax liability, or responsibility. There are

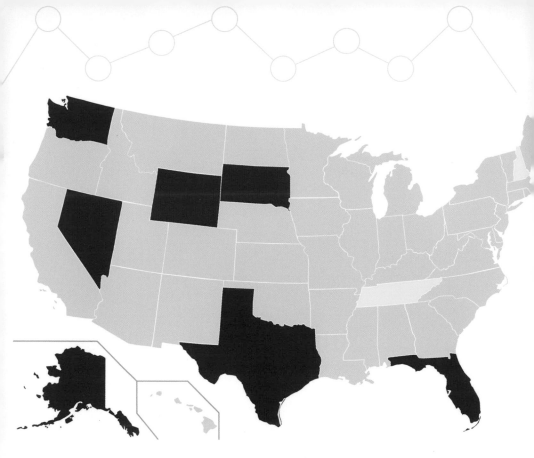

The states highlighted in red don't have a state income tax. The two highlighted in yellow don't either, although these do tax citizens' incomes from investments.

certain exemptions and deductions people qualify for when they file their annual taxes. An exemption is a standard amount of money you can subtract from your income. You can subtract this amount for having dependents, which are people for whom you are financially responsible. For instance, your parents probably claim you as a dependent, which gives them an exemption. Deductions are personal expenses that the government allows you to subtract from your income. These might include educational, medical, and business expenses, among others.

Where Your Money Goes

Each person's taxes support programs that are offered by federal, state, and local governments. People pay for these services even if they don't use them. For instance, a person with no children still helps to pay for schools. Taxpayers often complain about this. However, we don't just pay for the services we actually use. If that were the case, very few people would have the ability to afford these services.

Think about it like this: What if you had to pay the police department yourself every time you had to call 911? If your car got stolen, would you be able to afford the police services? What if you had to pay each time you drove your car on your own street? Someone has to maintain the roads, bridges, and streets that we drive on. What about the sewer and water systems in your town? Would you be willing to pay each time you turned on your faucet to wash your hands? If we all had to pay each time we used simple services, we'd never be able to afford to live our everyday lives.

TAXATION WITHOUT REPRESENTATION

Washington, DC, or the District of Columbia, is a district and is not recognized as a full-fledged state. For this reason, citizens of the District of Columbia do not have representation in the US Senate. The Senate is only made up of elected representatives from the fifty states. Despite the lack of representation, people in Washington, DC, still pay taxes. Over the years, a campaign has grown for the district to have senators who can represent its interests.

In November 2000, the DC Department of Motor Vehicles began issuing license plates with the slogan "Taxation Without Representation." In a show of support for the city, President Bill Clinton used the "Taxation Without Representation" plates on the presidential limousine during the final months of his presidency. The slogan speaks to the founding of the country, when the colonists fought for their independence from Great

Since plates with this slogan were issued in 2000, Presidents Bill Clinton, Barack Obama, and Donald Trump have used them on presidential limousines.

Britain based on the grounds that they were being taxed without having any say about the laws. In the early twenty-first century, people in the District of Columbia continue to push for full representation in Congress. Presidents have continued to use the license plate.

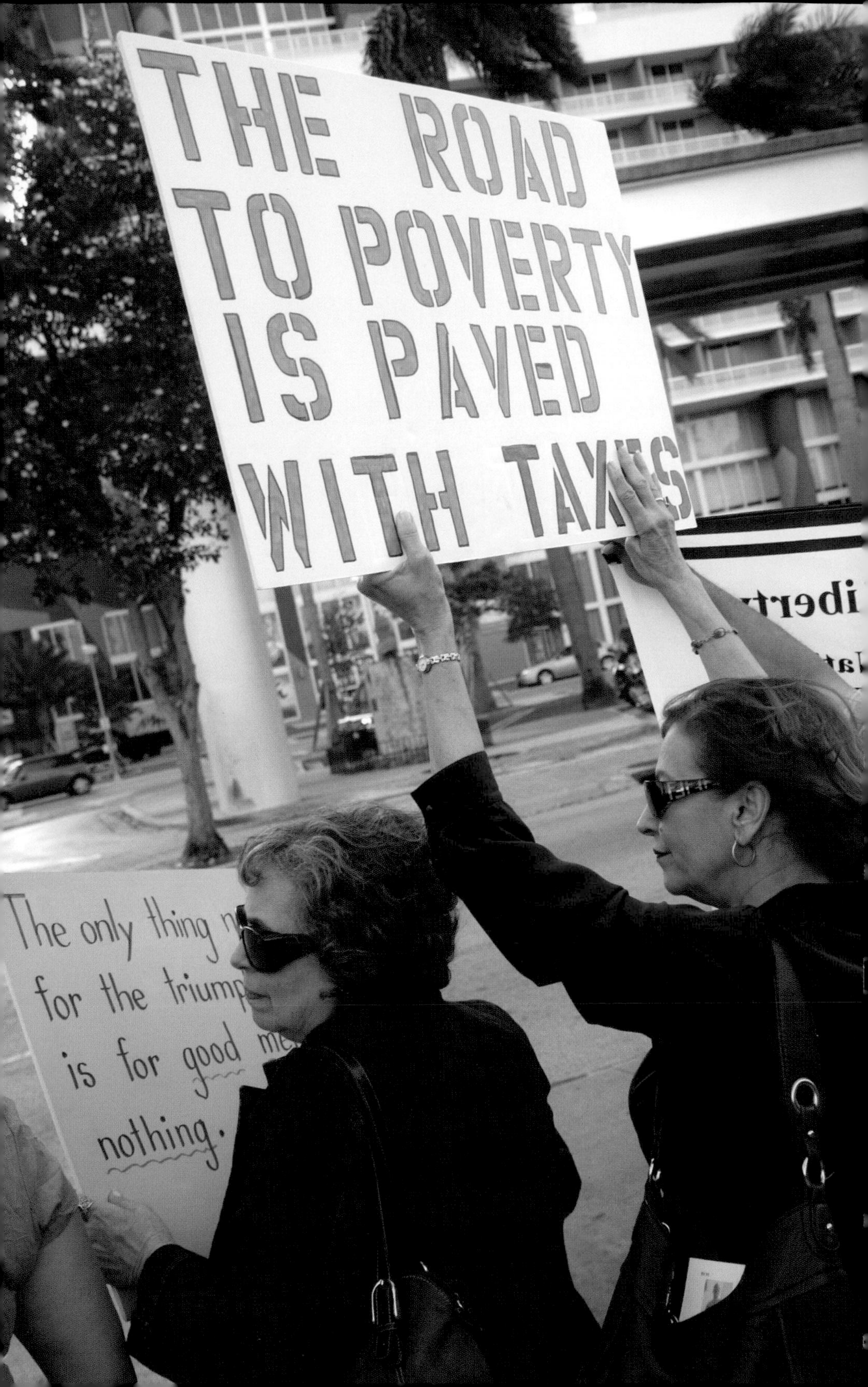
THE ROAD
TO POVERTY
IS PAVED
WITH TAX

CHAPTER 5

CHANGING TIMES

Not everyone agrees that we should pay taxes. In fact, there have been many attempts throughout history to protest or end taxation. Despite these sentiments, not many have offered alternative ways for the US government to earn money to pay for services that citizens use and need. The way US citizens pay taxes might change in the future. However, citizens will likely always pay taxes in some form.

An Early Protest

One colonial protest against taxation was the Boston Tea Party. Colonists were frustrated by the British tax on tea. Specifically, they thought the Tea Act violated their rights.

Opposite: A financially conservative group within the Republican Party called the Tea Party is adamant about the need for lowering taxes.

Many colonists believed they should be taxed only by representatives they elected to Parliament, Great Britain's governing body. They did not appreciate being ruled by a distant government. On December 16, 1773, after officials in Boston refused to return three shiploads of taxed tea to Britain, a group of colonists boarded the ships and destroyed the tea by throwing it into Boston Harbor. The event led to the American Revolution and a change in representation and taxes. However, it did not end taxation.

The Fair Tax Plan

There have been many proposed tax plans that could replace the federal and state income taxes we pay. One such idea is the Fair Tax Plan, which would replace all federal income tax with a single, national retail sales tax. Instead of paying taxes on the money you earn from your job, you would pay a higher sales tax on all items you buy.

Proponents of the plan say that there could be many positive outcomes from this new tax plan. For instance, financially challenged individuals would no longer have their income taxed, giving them more money to spend on what they saw fit. This may lead people to feel as though they have more control over the money they spend since the Fair Tax Plan is based on what consumers purchase. People who purchase fewer things would pay less money in taxes. Additionally, current government services would continue to be supported because, ideally, the money raised from a national sales tax would be equal to the amount of revenue earned from the federal income tax.

There are, however, many concerns about the Fair Tax Plan. Opponents to the plan say that less positive outcomes of the Fair Tax Plan could be that the price of goods and services would increase. Additionally, opponents are concerned that if the income tax is not fully abolished, a future president or Congress could reinstate part of the federal income tax program in response to a national emergency or crisis. This could result in Americans paying both a higher national sales tax and a federal income tax. The plan could also make it easier for the government to raise the tax rate on certain items that it deems unhealthy or dangerous, such as cigarettes, firearms, or junk food. People's concern with that is that the government would have too much influence over people's decisions.

People also object to the Fair Tax Plan because it's a regressive rather than progressive tax. This means people with lower incomes are disproportionally affected by the tax. The proponents of the plan, however, face this concern head on. They suggest sending people with lower incomes a prebate, or a monthly check, in order to offset the expenses related to the increased sales tax.

Tax Reform

Changing the way taxes work is called tax reform. Tax reformers, or the people who want to make the changes, are interested in changing the way taxes are collected and managed, reducing the amount of taxes people pay, and making the tax system easier to understand. Today, people try to reform the tax system by passing new laws. However, one of the first US tax reform efforts was the Whiskey Rebellion of 1794, which turned violent.

The Whiskey Rebellion occurred when President George Washington decided to tax whiskey to help pay off the country's national debt from the American Revolution. The tax was imposed on people who produced the whiskey but not the people who purchased it. Farmers thought the tax was unfair because they normally converted their excess grain into liquor as part of their livelihood. Tensions grew out of control as farmers and other supporters protested and attacked tax collectors. Washington sent 12,950 troops to western Pennsylvania, near Pittsburgh, to put an end to the rebellion. The Whiskey Rebellion is just one of the many events in history in which the people have tried to reform the tax system.

Despite the upheaval that some tax reforms can cause, it's not uncommon for the government to make changes to its tax policies. For instance, there have been over

People frustrated with the tax on whiskey tarred and feathered tax collectors to show their displeasure.

twenty major changes to tax legislation since 2000. These have not ended in bloodshed. For instance, people filing their 2018 tax returns in 2019 faced some of the biggest tax changes in federal income tax rules in nearly thirty years. Many of these changes revolved around expenses that were no longer tax-deductible. When an expense is tax-deductible, it can be subtracted from your tax liability, or the total income that you are responsible for

A FEW MORE FACTS

- *You can be audited even if you receive a tax refund.*
  Receiving your refund just means the IRS has reviewed your tax return and agreed with your calculations. That doesn't mean it won't go back to check that your filing is complete and accurate. The IRS can audit a return up to three years after it is received.

- *A tax preparer or accountant is not liable for mistakes on your tax forms.*
  The only person responsible for your tax documents is you, no matter who prepared them. Many taxpayers believe that if they use a professional accountant, that person is held responsible for any errors or omissions. Even if your accountant made a mistake, you will still need to pay for it. For that reason, it's incredibly important to choose a trustworthy and thorough tax professional.

paying taxes on. For many years, for example, moving expenses and job-search expenses were tax-deductible. After January 1, 2019, those were no longer necessarily the case. People expressed frustration about owing more; however, responses did not escalate to Whiskey Rebellion status. The reality is there will always be new proposals for how to collect taxes, and people who are not pleased with these changes.

Tax-Free Living

What would a country look like if its citizens paid no taxes? Can we live in a tax-free society? There have been organizations and groups that have suggested that we end the current taxation system and adopt a tax-free society in the United States. These groups have suggested many ways to create this system. One proposal is for every person to donate a certain amount of money to a trust fund. A trust fund is an account to which money is added and the interest is paid to the party named on the trust. In this case, the American people would donate money to a trust. The government would receive money from the trust to support the operation of the government.

Suppose we lived in a society without taxation. If there were no taxes, the government would not earn any income from taxation and citizens would not spend their hard-earned money on taxes. If someone had a wage of

The Cayman Islands is one of several countries that do not collect income or property taxes.

$10 an hour, he or she would be able to keep the entire amount. Many people in support of a society without taxation think that if taxation did not exist, people would spend more money. Maybe they would even work harder, knowing that they could keep every cent they earned.

There are a few countries that have tax-free societies. The Cayman Islands, a British territory located in the

Caribbean Sea, does not impose income or property taxes. The country's government raises money through taxes placed on importing and exporting goods, fees charged to tourists, work permit fees, and transaction fees. The Cayman Islands, however, is a much smaller country than the United States. In 2017, the Cayman Islands had about 60,000 people, compared to the over 325 million people living in the United States. The country also thrives off the fees it charges tourists, as the island saw over two million visitors in 2017 alone.

The Future

While there are many different systems of taxation in the world, every one of them has its pros and cons. It may not be a perfect system, but the US government has stuck to this current tax system because it has been working. If and when the government feels that it isn't, it will propose new laws and develop a new system. The country has done it at least once; it can do it again.

GLOSSARY

audit A review of your tax return by the IRS, during which you may be asked to prove that you have correctly reported your income, deductions, and exemptions.

debt Something that is owed, such as money, goods, or services.

deduction An expense you are permitted to subtract from your taxable income before figuring your tax bill.

exemption An amount of income excused from taxation.

Federal Insurance Contributions Act (FICA) An act which taxes people's paychecks to provide funding for Social Security and Medicare.

flat tax A standard rate of taxation that everyone pays, such as sales tax.

income The amount of money you earn.

Internal Revenue Service (IRS) The United States' tax collection agency.

progressive tax A tax in which the tax rate increases as the taxable amount increases.

revenue The income of a government from taxes and other sources.

sales tax A tax charged at the time of purchase for certain goods and services.

tariff A tax imposed on goods when they are moved across a political boundary.

tax bracket A division by which the amount of income taxes you pay is defined.

tax evasion Avoiding taxes intentionally, and by using illegal tactics.

tax liability The total amount an individual or business owes to the government in taxes.

tax reform The process of changing the way taxes are organized, collected, and managed by the government.

tax return A document filed by a taxpayer that gives the government an outline of what he or she owes in taxes for a given year.

withholding The amount held back from your paycheck that is used to pay your income and Social Security taxes.

FURTHER INFORMATION

Books

Bissinger, Caleb. *Taxes and Society's Priorities*. Introducing Issues With Opposing Viewpoints. New York: Greenhaven Publishing, 2018.

Currie, Stephen. *Teen Guide to Jobs and Taxes*. Teen Guide to Finances. San Diego: ReferencePoint Press, 2016.

Marcovitz, Hal. *The American Revolution*. Cause & Effect in History. San Diego: ReferencePoint Press, 2015.

Townsend, Chris. *What Does a Taxpayer Do?* What Does a Citizen Do? New York: Enslow Publishing, 2018.

Websites

EconEdLink

https://www.econedlink.org

This website, supported by the Council for Economic Education, provides economics and personal finance resources for teachers and students.

Investopedia

https://www.investopedia.com

This website features a wealth of information on financial and economic concepts.

SmartAsset

https://smartasset.com

This website provides free personal finance tools and resources like tax calculators to help you better understand how your paychecks are affected by taxes.

Videos

Taxes: Crash Course Economics #31

https://www.youtube.com/watch?v=7Qtr_vA3Prw

This video provides an overview of types of taxes, tax brackets, and some historical examples of responses to changes in tax policies.

Teens 'n Taxes: What's a W-4 form?

https://www.youtube.com/watch?v=oKLtwk_Jh6o

This video briefly explains a W-4 form, tax withholding, and how the government uses the money withheld.

Organizations

Americans for Fair Taxation
PO Box 4929
Clearwater, FL 33758
(800) 324-7829
Website: http://www.fairtax.org

Founded in 1995, Americans for Fair Taxation is a nonprofit organization dedicated to replacing the United States' current tax system with the Fair Tax Plan.

Canada Revenue Agency

Commissioner of Revenue
7th Floor
555 MacKenzie Avenue
Ottawa, ON K1A 0L5
Canada
(800) 959-8281
Website: https://www.canada.ca/en/revenue-agency.html

This Canadian agency is responsible for tax laws and the various public programs that the revenue from taxes supports.

Canadian Tax Foundation

145 Wellington Street West
Suite 1400
Toronto, ON M5J 1H8
Canada
(416) 599-0283
Website: http://www.ctf.ca

This foundation, which is well-regarded by the Canadian government, focuses on current tax issues and the improvement of the tax system.

Council on State Taxation

122 C Street NW
Suite 330
Washington, DC 20001
(202) 484-5222
Website: http://www.cost.org

The Council on State Taxation is a state tax organization, which represents and protects taxpayers.

Internal Revenue Service

1111 Constitution Ave NW
Washington, DC 20224
(202) 622-5000
Website: http://www.irs.gov

The Internal Revenue Service is the United States' tax collection agency.

Tax Foundation

1325 G St NW
Suite 950
Washington, DC 20005
(202) 464-6200
Website: http://www.taxfoundation.org

The mission of the Tax Foundation is to "improve lives through tax policies that lead to greater economic growth and opportunity."

SELECTED BIBLIOGRAPHY

American Institute of Certified Public Accountants. "Tax Reform Alternatives for the 21st Century." AICPA.org, October 2009. https://www.aicpa.org/Advocacy/Tax/DownloadableDocuments/Tax%20Reform%20Alternatives%202009.pdf.

Boortz, Neal, and John Linder. *The Fair Tax Book: Saying Goodbye to the Income Tax and the IRS.* New York: Harper Paperbacks, 2006.

Colonial Williamsburg. "A Summary of the 1765 Stamp Act." History.org. Accessed December 11, 2018. http://www.history.org/history/teaching/tchcrsta.cfm.

Cook, Colin. "How High Are Cigarette Tax Rates in Your State?" Tax Foundation, January 25, 2018. https://taxfoundation.org/state-cigarette-tax-rates-2018.

Ebeling, Ashlea. "IRS Official Audit Rate Down but the 'Real' Audit Rate Is the Problem." *Forbes*, March 29, 2018. https://www.forbes.com/sites/ashleaebeling/2018/03/29/irs-official-audit-rate-down-but-the-real-audit-rate-is-the-problem/#2dc0b5c31f92.

"The History of Income Taxes." Internal Revenue Service. Accessed December 21, 2018. https://www.irs.com/articles/the-history-of-income-taxes.

"Importance of Taxes: Why Should We Pay Tax to the Government?" Saching.com, June 18, 2009. http://www.saching.com/Article/Importance-of-taxes--Why-should-we-pay-tax-to-the-government/2682.

Rose, Jeff. "The New 2019 Federal Income Tax Brackets and Rates." *Forbes*, December 5, 2018. https://www.forbes.com/sites/jrose/2018/12/05/tax-brackets-and-rates-2019/#c90ed6c3ec50.

Schoen, John W. "How the Government Spends Your Taxes." MSNBC.com, April 3, 2008. http://www.nbcnews.com/id/23924282/ns/business-personal_finance/t/how-government-spends-your-taxes/#.XEviC6eZNQI.

INDEX

Page numbers in **boldface** refer to images.

ABOUT THE AUTHOR

Chet'la Sebree is a writer, editor, and researcher. She has written and edited several books for Cavendish Square Publishing, including one on the Great Depression. She has degrees in English and creative writing from the University of Richmond and American University, respectively. She is from the Mid-Atlantic region.